OVERC STUPID

in the world around us

The Stupid Aid Survival Guide

By Andy Green

**Illustrations and cover design
Joe Whittaker**

Published 2008 by the Flexible Thinking Forum, an imprint
of Tangent Books

Unit 5.16 Paintworks
Arnos Vale
Bristol
BS4 3EH

0117 972 0645
www.tangentbooks.co.uk

Publisher: Richard Jones richard@tangentbooks.co.uk
Design: David Oakley dave@arnosdesign.co.uk

Contents

Why this book?

It was when I was in a restaurant and asked for a slice of lemon for my drink. The young waitress apologized saying they didn't serve sliced lemon. Asking why, and after some gentle persistence, I was told: *"If we were to slice lemons we would have to use a knife and would then have to do a formal risk assessment. So we don't slice lemons."*

My drink remained un-lemoned, and I thought what a stupid organization to make that sort of decision and put their staff in such stupid situations.

I was also touched with a sense that somehow this was not a one-off incident but actually part of something more prevalent; indeed, an insidious threat to the quality of modern-day life.

This guide is written for anyone who has experienced their own examples of my lemon moment. It leads to the questions: is the world getting more stupid, or is there too much stupidity around us?

This guide also explains why, in spite of massive technological advances to make us act 'smarter', the opposite seems to happen.

While there are many books highlighting many different aspects of the absurdities of modern life, this is perhaps a first in providing practical help to do something about it.

The book is a call to arms to use its inspiration, tools, and ideas to fight back, combat, or feel not so helpless when confronted with stupidity.

Whether it is dealing with bureaucrats, your boss, or when the buck stops with you, this book will help you.

Ultimately, we are all capable of stupidity: Daily we experience the ''Doh' factor', where we have done something stupid. At the very least this book will make you feel more comfortable about your daily stupidity - so long as you avoid what it labels 'five star stupidity'.

Whether you want to support *'Stupid Aid – to make stupidity history'* (see pages 125-6 for the story of Stupid Aid), or just want to boost your flexible thinking, creativity and opportunity spotting skills – to make your bit of the world a better place – this is an essential survival guide.

Part One

(or Part 3 if you are reading in reverse order)

Stupidity at large

What do we mean by 'stupidity', and is the world getting more stupid?

What's causing an increase in stupidity? Are we all 'stupid'?

The dictionary defines 'stupidity' as: 'foolish or unwise; lacking judgment or intelligence, dull by nature, slow-witted, lacking in sensibility.'. (The word 'stupid' derives from the Latin 'stupidus' meaning numb or stunned.)

Yet we all know of incredibly clever or able people who do stupid things or make stupid decisions. Even the smartest of lives are not without their episodes of stupidity.

Was Field Marshal Haig stupid when he sent thousands of British and Commonwealth soldiers to certain death in the battlefields of France?

 Or Sir Isaac Newton, the eminent scientist, who spent much of his life obsessed with the fruitless study of alchemy.

Or the former American President, Bill Clinton in his dealings with a Ms. Lewinsky?

These people were not of low intelligence.

They are not who we would traditionally call 'stupid'. But were guilty of stupid actions and decisions.

We need to fundamentally redefine stupidity. Stupidity is about making choices which don't add value. They create negative value which makes the world a worse place to live, work, or raise our children.

It is not caused by low intelligence – as evidenced from the examples above. Rather it should be defined as being caused by inappropriate inflexible thinking, without asking questions, which don't add value. It is the inflexibility of thinking which leads to stupidity.

If there was such a thing as Stupidity Quotient it would be a measure not of the inherent qualities of a person. It would instead be a measure on their behaviours. As a certain Forrest Gump observed: 'Stupid is as stupid does'.

The first step in any effective treatment of a problem is to accurately define and describe it.

By more specifically defining stupidity as being caused by inflexible thinking we get around the stigma associated with the word 'stupid'. It's not about abusing people of low intelligence.

Indeed, the opposite is the case; if we succeed in taking the word 'stupid' away from those who should more accurately regarded as having 'special needs' – we can fully grasp the problem of 'compound stupidity' (a stupid act based on an earlier stupid idea) in the world at large.

By removing the pejorative 'stupid' away from a group of people who need understanding, support, and compassion, matched with respect, I believe it also helps their situation.

Where do we start in tackling the growth in stupidity in the world around us?

I'm going to put my hand up here and admit to being stupid.

I have some rather stupid beliefs.

Like, I am not the most lightweight person around, so when it comes to addressing my efforts to weigh less I am not helped by believing 'it's not fair', 'I don't seem to eat that much'. Somehow, I just have to look at food to put on weight.

I have stupid behaviours. Stupidly, I support a football team called West Ham United FC, where I believe we are one of the best teams around. I go to matches convinced we are going to win. At least they are consistent. They consistently let me down.

I have done stupid things. All of us can recall a significant cock up at work where you have done stupid.

As a young public relations officer I was once editor of a fishing magazine (it's a long story.) I did not know one end of a fish from another. This ignorance got me into hot water with anglers when I ran a fun photo caption competition.

It featured a photo of a young angler posing to tuck into a giant Pike he had caught, and not returned to the water. A golden rule for any basic knowledge angler is that once you catch fish, such as Pike, you return them back to the water, to live another day. It is taboo to do otherwise. I did not have basic knowledge.

The response from anglers was not mild to say the least. The front page lead in the 'Angling Times' (this was a publication which then had over 100,000 readers) screamed out about 'ANGLERS IN OUTRAGE' featuring the immortal quote from one anglers' representative, claiming the competition was, 'as funny as a concentration camp'.*

Admit it, We've all done stupid things in our work.

(*This story is actually an example of 3 star stupidity – see page 28)

In my youth I listened to radio DJ Johnny Walker who hosted 'Pop the question', a lunchtime phone-in music quiz on BBC Radio 1. I recall being astonished at how 'thick' one contestant was who didn't know what the then Number 1 record in the charts was.

Many years on, I must admit haven't got the faintest idea who, or what is number 1 in the charts.

Have I grown 'thicker'?

All of us have areas of ignorance. It can change over time. We are all different with our varying degrees of expertise and ignorance. Inevitably, to some people, at some time, we will be 'stupid'.

This we will discover is what is called 1 star stupidity.

With the rapid growth in knowledge, (note, this is not a growth in smartness) we all will know less and less about more and more.

We are living in an age of rapid change, where the rate of change is spiraling faster and faster.

You find if you work in an office you can't just answer your phone. You have to check your emails at the same time.

On a recent trip to New York's Central Park I saw a guy jogging, pushing a baby in a pram and reciting the times table to his passive protégé.

I suppose all of us are like the baby in the New York pram. We live in an age of information obesity where we no longer have time to do just one thing at one time.

We multi-task as one coping mechanism against being inundated with information and the intensive demands upon our precious time. (How many of us who work in offices read our e mails while dealing with a phone call – and make stupid mistakes as a result?)

We also cope by pushing the instant solution button to any problem we face and move on, focused on heading off the next missive to come our way.

The satirical magazine *'Private Eye'* collects examples of what it calls 'Dumb Britain' where people give stupid responses or make stupid comments on quiz shows or in the media.

My favourite is the quizmaster who asked: *"What happened in Dallas in 1963?"*

The contestant answered: *"I don't know. I didn't watch the show then."*

Or what about: *"Which breakfast cereal is also slang for a period of imprisonment?"*

"Cheerios" was the answer given.

Although you can laugh at these examples, the people who committed the gaffes were not necessarily stupid. They gave a stupid response under the pressure of limited time. They had to give an instant answer in an unrelenting situation.

How much is real-life starting to mirror the quiz show, where you only have 10 seconds to make up your mind?

A Cumbrian man in April 2008 was fined, and now possesses a criminal record for over-filling his rubbish bin.

Evidently, he was a perfectly law-biding citizen, who was following everything by the book by putting his waste in his appointed wheelie-bin. His mistake was to over-fill it, which presumably made it more hassle for the collectors, and ran contrary to the valid need for all of us to reduce the waste we create so lessening our impact on the earth's precious resources.

Sure, our society, and our agents for waste collection need to bring about a change of behaviours, so each and every one of us produces less waste. But is making someone, who otherwise is a supporter of your system, a criminal the right way to go about this?

What about leaving excess waste in the bin, to provide feedback and indicate the person has produced too much waste that week with less capacity for the following week's waste. Could ideas such as exploring ways for excess charging, or education lessons been explored. There must have been an alternative, anything other than making someone a criminal.

For people in power, their ability to dispense penalties is easily discharged. They wouldn't dream, one would hope, of bringing back the death penalty if your library books are overdue. Yet they are being blind to wider consequences of their actions: the potential public backlash, bad PR, in this case, the fostering of a resentment about what is being labelled a 'Green Taliban' or 'Green Gestapo', are all potential negatives, albeit not tangible – they don't get on the phone to warn of their possible arrival.

We are witnessing something we can label as 'organizational autism'* - a mind blindness, an inability to understand human nature, to get in the heads of other people and understand how they see the world – and its difference to ours. It seems like people are abdicating responsibility and jumping at the opportunity to stop thinking.

This shying away from the complexity of a challenge, taking the easy solution, and absolute conviction in your own systems, are symptoms of compound stupidity.

(*My younger brother is autistic and I feel it is quite politically correct to use the word in this way.)

During my first Stupid Aid tour of 2007 I asked audiences for examples of stupidity they recently encountered.

My favourite story came from someone who related how their sister had a car accident where another vehicle had run into the side of her. The other driver leapt out apologizing with the excuse: *"I'm sorry, my Satnav [Satellite navigation system] didn't show the T junction!"*

The story seems to echo similar experiences we all have of being victims of technology. I wanted to book a doctor's appointment for three weeks hence, on my return from a fortnight's break. The doctor's receptionist's computer system however, would only allow for appointments to be made up to two weeks ahead, and was impossible to schedule one beyond that.

The technology was seemingly getting in the way of common sense. It was creating stupid situations. It is accompanied by a sense of omniscience among people who administer systems. They seemingly feel they have complete control over all the potential variables they face. This leads to a sense of managers believing they know much more than do.

Stupidity in the world is further assisted by the faster speed of negative word of mouth.

One of my favourite cartoons depicts three male students wearing T-shirts. The younger two have shirts proclaiming *'Ban the bomb'* and *'Save the Whale'*. The elder among the trio has a shirt with the message *'...it's a bit more complicated than that'*. Beneath the image is a caption where the two younger men mutter: *"Don't you hate mature students!"*

The reality is that most issues – and their solutions – are usually not black or white, but reside in varying shades of grey. They are more complex and intractable, beyond salvation by just a simple slogan.

Word-of-mouth – how messages can spread like wildfire - works most effectively where there is a clear-cut, 'sticky' message which is memorable, easy-pass-onable, and is easily accommodated in someone's worldview. (A posh word for this word-of-mouth dynamic is 'memes' – pass it on.)

So when you see stories such as those about so-called 'loony councils' or organizations making daft decisions, particularly on grounds of 'health and safety' or 'data protection', they often may not be true, or are severely distorted in the telling.

And because the resulting tale is usually neat, snappy, memorable, and makes us feel more comfortable in some way, they get passed on. The more complex, convoluted truth can often not even get to first base while a sticky untruth is halfway around the world.

In a super networked world, with word-of-click viral emails operating like 'word-of-mouth on speed', stupidity travels even faster.

As a result the messages which get relayed – 'you will get sued or fined if you do this', or easy opt-out excuses like 'health and safety' or 'data protection' get passed on. All fuelling the potential for more stupidity.

Why is the world getting more stupid?

We are witnessing 'compound stupidity' where stupidity feeds itself at a faster rate.

This has come about because people and decision-makers are failing to cope with:

- Faster pace of life, speed of development, and communications
- Greater complexity of the world
- Lower cost of 'logical' technologies – such as databases and on-line procedures, accompanied by an unlimited faith of users with their 'system', making them used more widely, and often inappropriately. They fail to take account of the illogical nature of emotions and the random, haphazard reality of the real world.
- Negative word-of-mouth traveling faster than positive, so people are often basing decisions on imbalanced information.

In its 2007 Stupid Aid survey people were asked: *'Is the world getting more stupid?'* Yes, was the reply. (Admittedly, it was a highly subjective response from a limited sample. It did provide some confirmation of recognition of 'compound stupidity' in modern life.)

One of the big friends of increasing stupidity in the world, as we shall explore shortly, is people's inherent laziness, to opt for the superficially attractive easy, quick solutions.

In the short-term it can be more secure and less stressful to hide behind someone else's rules or instant decision. (Although this ultimately may be more stressful in the long-term.)

I once did a creativity session with a leading local authority library service. I explained that although I thought the service is brilliant, my lifestyle militates against getting books back on time. It resulted in persistent fines anytime I borrowed a book.

When appealing for more flexibility in their system, the head librarian explained that they had tried to give staff more discretion, but in the end, at the insistence of the staff, reverted back to a well-defined regime of fixed schedules and fines for late returners: staff wanted the security and comfort of not having to make a decision.

Most people will recognise the 'call centre syndrome' where any 'off-script' requests face frustrations of an un-yielding wall of bureaucracy as organizations fail to cope with what appears a simple, straight-forward task.

We daily witness, or read about examples of stupid thinking, whether it is government, council decisions, big business, or the growth of 'nonebrity'* culture.

*Someone who is famous for no outstanding quality.

We are witnessing an era of growing technical sophistication outstripping the human dimension of people's decision-making abilities in a more complex, faster-moving world.

The two dynamics are often out-of-synch. The greater technical proficiency can often exacerbate the effects of stupid decision-making and ultimately lead to even more counter-productive situations.

This combines with our individual efforts to reduce dissonance – the anxious uneasy feeling you get after making a new decision, caused by still being uncertain if you made the right the choice. To cope with complexity around us we use avoidance, denial, or imposing false realities to make our current worldview more tolerable.

It is easier to hide behind someone else's rule – the orders from above – rather than create dissonance for us.

But stupidity knows no hiding place.

Everything is uncertain in the universe

The need for a comfort blanket, of a world full of certainty, what can be called 'secureness' is an understandable goal. Yet is there any certainty in our universe?

Scientists were faced with a conundrum when examining the very essence of matter. If they were trying to say measure a gas, for example, the electrons would be in different places at different times. It was like trying to pin down water.

They overcome this challenge by introducing the concept of probability; it didn't matter where the precise, exact location of a particular piece of matter was, so long as it could fall within an agreed range of probability. This would be sufficient for the scientist to map out and manage the precise detail of matter.

So, even at the very centre of our universe we witness uncertainty, and how things are never constant nor immovable.

If nature works like that, why can't we? Why do we have organizations with absolutely rigid rules?

Isn't that stupid?

By Jove, it gets even more complicated ...

I once foolishly sat in the front row at a show by comedian Ken Dodd. His act featured picking on different members of the audience. *'You sir, what is your surname?'* he asked. On being told it was *'Green'* he said: *"Do you know that means handsome, generous and kind?"* He then enquired about my first name: *'Andy'* he concluded, means *"Not very."*

No matter how wonderful or brilliant you think you, or your ideas are, their value is defined and determined by its context.

We also live in a world of infinite complexity. On my creativity training courses I use a technique inspired by American creative Jack Foster of asking delegates what is half of 13? (Try it now as an exercise.)

The real answer is that there is an infinite number of answers, with responses given on my courses ranging from 6.5 to half of one delegate's dog who was called '13'!

Yet, our expanding regime of computer-based linear logic based systems leads us into a deluded world that somehow everything is exact, precise, manageable, controllable and any potential risk can be met by a defined prescription.

It is a world where individuals or organizations perceive their 'Plan' as perfect, whether it is a system for making sure people don't overfill their bins, to blindly driving our cars by Satnav only. They ignore the reality of 'stuff happens'

We live in a world which is made up of an infinite amount of data. We succeed at times in translating some of this data into information. It is your ability to deduce 'meaning', the critical insight from this information, that enables you to make intelligent assessments and decisions.

No matter how many facts you have at your fingertips, you need to have meaning in your mind - a sense of what it all adds up to – to overcoming stupidity.

We will discover later how bureaucrats are actually being creative when they say 'No'.

It is stupid to think you can anticipate every potential outcome in a world full of infinite complexity, where the value of any action is determined by its context.

5 star stupidity – why all stupidity is not the same

To help us manage how we deal with stupidity in all its forms it is useful to classify five different types of stupidity.

1 star	Stupid thinking is a one-off mistake, based on inaccurate, unbalanced, or insufficient information.
2 star	Stupid thinking failing to recognise wider community or partnership interests when making a decision.
3 star	Stupid thinking failing to recognise longer-term needs in the consequences of the decision.
4 star	Applying 1, 2 or 3 star stupid thinking in new areas of activity leading to 'compound stupidity'.
5 star	The ultimate, and least forgivable act of stupidity, repeatedly making the same 1,2 3 or 4 star mistakes.

All of us inevitably will generate what is 1, 2 or 3 star stupidity in our lives.

1 star stupidity growth

The universe of knowledge is ever expanding at an exponential rate. Humans have a finite capacity to absorb and contain information. Inevitably, we will know less and less of what there is to know.

Sure, this will be countered to some degree by our using greater networking – particularly on-line (such as the growth in people using their mobile phones to surreptitiously Google in a pub quiz!). Like in the examples of the stupid quiz contestants on page 13, you cannot always Google your way out of a situation.

The fundamental remains, of more and more data, being dealt with by a device, our minds – a piece of kit originally fashioned in the Stone Age.

The logic of this is how we will increasingly make less than optimum decisions. These decisions may often suffice in meeting the basic needs of the problem. In a wider context however, with other better quality options available, the decision will be evidently stupid.

2 star stupidity growth
With greater complexity in the world there inevitably will be actions producing unexpected and unintended consequences in different situations.

On a business trip to Dubai I read in the local paper about a consumer boycott of the 'Dunkin Donuts' fast food chain. The cause: In the United States a consumer protest led to the dropping of an advert featuring a gentleman with Arabian headgear because it somehow 'promoted terrorism'. In the Middle East however, such a response provoked a different negative of being 'anti-Arab'. The local 'Dunkin Donut' franchise in Dubai appealed in vain that the decision was nothing to do with them – it was the stupidity of head office in the United States.

3 star stupidity growth

With the faster rate of change it produces a consequence of people looking for instant solutions. I want it, and I want it now! The consequence will be of greater short-term answers, which over a period of time will look stupid, whether it is building houses on flood plains (there might be a clue in the name there!) to our society getting the politicians it deserves who avoid difficult issues over pensions, the environment, and energy needs.

4 stupidity growth

With the surge in 1, 2, and 3 star stupidity it will fuel the growth of 4 star 'compound stupidity', of one stupid idea feeding another. As the song by the band Tickled Pink goes: 'Somebody has a bad idea, somebody makes it worse, compound stupidity the 21st century curse.'

5 star stupidity

This is one stupidity we can do something about – not to repeat a bad idea, act, or rule. Doing 5 star stupidity is stupid.

Perhaps you are stupid too

Until Stupid Aid, using the word 'stupid' was too black and white, too emotive, and too blunt to provide a practical tool in managing the stupidity around you.

Once you embrace the idea of stupidity - based on inflexible thinking with five types of stupidity - and how everyone inevitably does stupidity, this gives you a set of tools to enter into a dialogue about discussing your own and other people's stupidity.

Once, other people embrace these ideas you start overhearing phrases like, *"I guess that might be a case of two star and certainly three star stupidity"* or, *"I hold my hand up, it was one star stupidity – I wasn't aware of the other option."*

Equally, it is far more damning to accuse someone of four or five star stupidity because they need to respond using logic, to explain their reasons behind why they did something. They need to either reverse their decision or justify their course of action.

Before the advent of Stupid Aid, if you called something 'stupid' it would make any dialogue emotionally charged. People start digging holes to defend their position rather than explore, through a scale of options, to get to the root cause of the issue.

Once you get over the stigma associated with stupid actions, and recognise it is an almost inevitable feature of your daily life then you can actually start tackling the consequences of your thinking, rather than be hung up about if you are 'stupid' or not. (Flexible thinking also means you should celebrate your moments of brilliance each day, and don't just get hung up on the negative.)

Isn't it stupid to go into denial about your own stupidity?

Your flexible thinking friend

Well, you now have the start of an intellectual framework to address stupidity in the world at large. With your active support and engaging others, these ideas could emerge as the conventional thinking of our age. It beats our current option of having an emotive word 'stupid' to be used in extreme occasions.

You will need more than this if you are going to tackle stupidity in the world at large or in your own backyard.

If we define stupidity as being caused by inappropriate inflexible thinking, then to address this challenge each of us need to develop our muscles in flexible thinking.

I define creativity as:
'Flexible thinking around beautiful questions in a quest to add value'.

Recalling our earlier definition of 'stupidity' as inflexible thinking, without asking questions, to create negative value, you can see how creativity is the nemesis of stupid thinking.

The creative act is not necessarily about coming up with 1001 different ideas. At its heart is identifying the right question – the beautiful question – and to flexibly think around that.

We all should be on a quest to make things better, hence the notion of added value. We should use our thinking to improve things or offset the impact of stupid thinking.

Flexible thinking is a key component of creativity. And the good news is that we are all brilliant creativity machines ...

There is no such thing as a creative/uncreative person ...

My work in giving talks at conferences often involves me leaving our home in Yorkshire at 5am to get the train to London. One day, on arriving in the capital, I found a message on my mobile phone from my wife simply saying: *"Just calling to say 'Hello'."*

Touched, I called back only to discover she had already set off for work.

Now, I am not normally a romantic guy, (so I'm not letting down any male readers out there), but thought the gesture of having a single rose with a card saying 'Hello' would be a nice reply.

I rang her local florist and was told they could deliver flowers to my wife's school that morning. I was politely asking for a single rose with a card, when the florist interrupted: *"We only deliver bouquets."*

I weighed up the situation. A bouquet would, I felt, be a bit over-the-top, not in keeping with the simple message I wanted to deliver. I then asked: *"Could I have a single rose within the bouquet?"*

On hearing I could, I gave the florist precise instructions: *"After putting the rose with a card saying 'Hello' in the bouquet, before you get to the exit of your shop put all the flowers, except the rose, in the bin - and then proceed on your journey."*

Clearly, the florist was guilty of defining her job as 'Delivering bouquets of flowers'.

I defined her job in a much wider context of 'Deliverer of emotional messages.'

Yet, I too was guilty of not seeing things in a wider context; I was paying the same for a single rose as I was for a bouquet. (I am reckoned to be one of the tightest people in Yorkshire - you may be familiar with the definition of a Yorkshireman as 'a Scotsman stripped of his generosity'.)

Maybe, with a bit of sweet talking I could have persuaded the florist to deliver the rose and the bouquet to the school, with the other flowers to be given to my wife's colleague as a 'thank you' for looking after our dog during a recent holiday.

This inappropriate narrowness of thinking is something that affects all of us. I will later demonstrate how even bureaucratic thinking has creative thought at its heart.

So, there is no such thing as a creative and non-creative person.

We all have a potential phenomenal resource to creatively respond to acts of stupidity.

We are all guilty of 'lazy thinking'

I have run several hundred creative thinking skills classes, and read several hundred texts on the subject. I go as far to describe myself as a 'mini global celebrity in a micro niche'. (I once lectured in Beijing where I met an American woman who had bought one my books in San Francisco, so I guess that stacks up my claim.)

The number one reason I have discovered why people are not fulfilling their creative potential, or organizations not buzzing with innovation, is not down to a lack of tools, processes, or un-supporting corporate cultures.

It's down to one key thing:

We are all lazy.

We are lazy when we are doing an idea session when we give up too soon in discovering and defining the right, beautiful questions. We are lazy when we are, what I call green light sparking off ideas and stop producing further ideas by saying to ourselves: *'I can't think of anything else'*.

We are lazy in the follow-through by not nurturing or developing ideas into realizable added value concepts or products.

Even 'blue sky thinking' is a lazy misnomer: the sky is not blue.

My wife once rang up a call centre on my behalf to change the details on my account only to be told they would only deal with me, because of 'data protection'.

Now data protection is a vital, fundamental measure. You don't want any Tom, Dick or Harriet knowing your personal details. Your privacy needs to be protected.

By refusing to deal with the request from my wife, the call centre was not actually compromising the Data Protection Act; my personal details were not being given out to a third party.

Sure, the call centre was actually adopting sensible customer information management, so protecting it against devious or unscrupulous acts, but it's not down to the Data Protection Act.

They are actually guilty of what is labelled 'duck out data protection' – using the term 'data protection' as a shield to hide behind, an excuse to duck out of really addressing the person's needs. It also fails to understand what data protection is, and perhaps when they should really be applying its principles.

What the call centre is really saying when it practises duck out data protection is: *'If you don't precisely approach us in the most efficient way for our system, we can't be bothered to help you.'*

If you label a problem as a 'monkey' and your having a problem is a 'monkey on your shoulder', a really good customer service would take the proverbial monkey off of your shoulder.

In reality these call centres should actually be re-branded customer dis-service centres.

In my example, the fact my wife calling was a signal from me, the customer, that I have a problem which needs attending to. They could for example have taken note of the request, done all they could, taking it as far as possible, and make it easy for me to formally sign-off or give a final instruction. But in this case, as it seems from many other people's experience, the monkey was resolutely left on our shoulders and she was told to go away.

Far too often it seems we are feeling frustration caused by the lazy thinking of others leading to lazy actions, and as a result, greater stupidity in the world around us.

So, what do you need to do overcome this laziness?

Part Two

Your toolbox

Each of us has a toolbox in our heads. In fact it's a brilliant toolbox with the capability of unleashing brilliant, original ideas, solutions and questions to make the world a better place.

Like any skill if you can embrace a number of key principles and adopt certain techniques you can be better equipped to face your challenges.

Part Two of this book shares some key principles and flexible thinking tools to help you tackle the stupidity around you – and overcome lazy thinking.

Principles 1: The 'Black Sock' syndrome

The first and foremost excuse for not getting anything done is 'I haven't got time?'

I have yet to meet anyone who says they have loads of spare time.

Whether you are challenging stupidity or coming up with new creative ideas, you will similarly face objections of 'You don't have enough time.'

It is inevitable that if you are exploring new ways of doing or taking up new challenges it will consume valuable time. So, the first task of either a Stupid Aid ambassador or creative person is to create time for themselves.

In my house I once had a thief. After doing the laundry I would find I would have odd socks missing. Where had they gone? Have they walked away, or been eaten? I just found it an incredible waste of my time acting as a sock dating agency matching up different socks together.

My solution: I now wear just black socks and get away with wearing socks that may not be an original pair, but being uniformly black, people don't seem to notice. The solution has generated sufficient added value to provide a solution to the problem, and I now have created more time for myself.

What is the equivalent of your 'black socks syndrome'? Where in your life can you save time on unnecessary or unimportant things? You can use this new spare time for either your new creative ideas or for tackling compound stupidity around you.

Principle 2: Be brave but wear a life jacket

I met a brilliant woman on one of my training events for social enterprises. She possessed great intensive energy and successfully had delivered some great initiatives to make the world a better place. She was however, troubled by an incident the previous week, where in making a complaint at a supermarket, the situation escalated to the police being called.

Still livid about the episode a week later, she felt she had been in the right, unfairly treated, and at the very least had also revealed shortcomings in the supermarket's customer complaints process.

Wanting my view on whether she should pursue the complaint I enquired what was important in her life; her social mission or getting a supermarket to change its procedures.

If you want to change the world make sure you choose your battles. You can't take everyone on. Your personal energy is a dynamic, wonderful resource to fuel your efforts to force change in the world. Like the earth's own energy reserves, use it wisely and focus on where your real passion is.

Whenever you are trying to launch a new idea or challenge a status quo you need to be brave. It's better to be brave wearing a life jacket though.

Make sure your battle is the right one and minimize the risk of being rejected. Have you done sufficient initial research to back your claims or investigate its potential robustness – the equivalent of wearing a life jacket?

Recognise that your pessimism is brilliant. It is a vital negative check to identify what can go wrong, what are the obstacles you need to overcome. But practice 'pit stop pessimism'.

Rather like a Formula 1 car you sometimes need to make a pit stop for your negativity. And like the racing car get out of the pit stop as soon as possible, make your stay there as short as is necessary for you to go on and successfully complete your journey.

You will need to be brave to embark on the journey of tackling stupidity, but remember to pack your life jacket.

Principle 3: Be the bigger person

I was once blessed with meeting Lord David Puttnam when he kindly agreed to come and formally open one of my businesses, a media centre in Wakefield.

Now, two key things about Lord Puttnam. He is a rightly, successful Oscar-winning film producer. He is also a great bloke.

In my creativity training I highlight how it is important to see the bigger picture, recognise a bigger context you and your creative challenge operate within, to give you more options, scope to explore different dimensions and alternatives.

What my encounter with Lord Puttnam revealed was how I was failing to live and be the bigger person as well as think the bigger horizons.

I had been guilty of what can be called 'blue arse flying'. I was always in a hurry. Conversations were snatched, e mails almost terse, and had to get straight away from meetings or events as there was inevitably something elsewhere seemingly more pressing in need of my attention.

For his visit we had arranged for Lord Puttnam to meet the media centre community and envisaged him just saying a courteous 'hello', shaking hands and then moving on. He upset our plans however.

Every one he met he appeared to show a genuine interest in and engaged with a more extended conversation about their situation, concerns and aspirations. People felt two foot taller after meeting him, and sensed they had met a brilliant person, a great bloke.

David Puttnam was demonstrating how you not only have to think the bigger picture but live and breathe the 'biggerness' with every connection or encounter you make. When meeting people it's not about gossiping all day, but introducing what I call 'the little linger' in your meeting; it is extending the conversation or e mail with a genuine interest in the other person's world.

You then find other people start rallying to your cause or show an interest in what you do, and may possibly help you in your cause, or to overcome stupidity.

Principle 4: Be the brand you ought to be

If you mention the word 'brand' most people associate it with consumer goods and names like 'Coca Cola', 'Microsoft' or 'Dolce & Gabbana'.

Yet, each and every one of us is a brand. The way people know of us, whether it is close relations or as a third hand minor celebrity is as a brand: our unique personality and complexity of what we are is reduced to a shorthand understanding of selected characteristics, attitudes, interests, and activities.

We are all personal brands. We are all mini celebrities in micro niches. You don't have a choice about whether to be a brand or not. What you can choose is whether to manage your brand to assist your life's mission in some way. Everyone should aspire to be a mega celebrity in their micro niche for the right reason.

This is not saying you have to be artificial and false. Indeed, a key quality of a brand is its need for integrity, a truthfulness about what is at the heart. Others will recognise if you are false, and eventually see through any insincere camouflage or packaging.

Your brand consists of three key elements:

Your icons – the instant things that people remember you for – your appearance, achievements, or associations.

Your values – which drive your behaviour and determine what gets done, and what doesn't.

A value you can define as something you do even when it hurts.

Far too often people and organizations posture about their 'values', and they can often amount to little more than empty platitudes, rather than real measures of who they are, what they stand for, and what they are prepared to die for. (As the publicity blurb for the Clint Eastwood film *'Flag of Glory'* about soldiers in Iwo Jima during World War II blurbed: 'They fought for their country but died for their friends. Their friends were the higher level value, not the patriotism)

Your information – the facts and details about yourself.

Great communicators come in all shapes and sizes. They all share the key characteristics of great 'Personal brandcasting' by doing four key things.

1. They have a strong sense of mission, who they are, what they stand for.

2. They communicate in every dimension of their life, by the way they dress, deal with other people and most importantly their actions: actions speak louder than words.

3. Great people create strong word of mouth, sticky messages or memes.

4. They create and maintain strong networks around them.

By making the most of your personal brand you are maximising the most of you, to help you take on the world – and stupidity.

Principle 5: Bring more variety to your life

If you want to see things differently you need to experience different things. Doing the 'usual', the routine, familiar makes life easy. You don't have to think, nor create new anxieties for your self by taking on new stuff.

By doing the usual, the routine, the familiar you also make it easy for stupidity.

Trying new things, breaking out of patterns you create for yourself makes your mind more mobile and agile in how it responds to new things. You have a wider pool of information and experience to draw upon. Your assumption making is less rigid. And you also expand your comfort zone.

Your comfort zone contains all the things you feel safe doing. Going outside your comfort zone, tackling the stuff that can make you anxious or unsure, helps expand the zone so you grow to accept as comfortable things previously thought difficult.

I once did a creativity session with some Polish students where I explained the comfort zone concept. *"Ah, zis is the secret of eternal youth"* remarked one of the group. *"What do you mean?"* I asked. *"We'll, Andy, if your comfort zone keeps growing you don't get older!"*

No matter how old and wrinkled you may be on the outside, if your comfort zone is expanding you grow younger within.

You don't need to be Indiana Jones to spice up your life. I have a lovely old friend Joe who lives in Leeds and I took him out for lunch in Wakefield, nine miles away. Afterwards, I told Joe I was dropping him off home. He declined the offer: *"No, it's alright, I will get the bus instead. It will be an adventure."*

Every day look out for three good and bad things relevant to what's important to you. Then deconstruct why they are good or bad. By doing so you are exercising your sagacity muscle, your ability, your radar to spot opportunities around you. (Sagacity I would define as doing now what you would have done in hindsight.)

Trying new things, whether it is a different newspaper, radio station, way to work, going first class or budget, where you sit at meetings, your waking up routine, your mood with different people, or random acts of kindness all expand your comfort zone – and make you younger, and help you overcome stupidity.

Principle 6: It's always a judgement call

One of my first tasks as a young public relations consultant was to produce a case study for a print equipment manufacturer by visiting and talking to printers using their products.

I was met with some frostiness by the first printer I called. I succeeded in getting the guy to open up and he shared with me his observation about advertising and public relations agencies: *"I hate agencies, because they always want everything and you can't have everything with a print job."*

He then proceeded to draw a triangle: *"Any print job has three dimensions. At one end of the triangle is cost, the apex is quality, and at the other end of the triangle is time. You can only score on one or two dimensions; if you want a quick job then there has to be a sacrifice in either cost or quality. If you want quality then you have to accept it may cost more or take longer to do. If you want a cheap job, then the quality or the time it takes may have to be compromised."*

"Agencies always want all three things at once. And that can't be done."

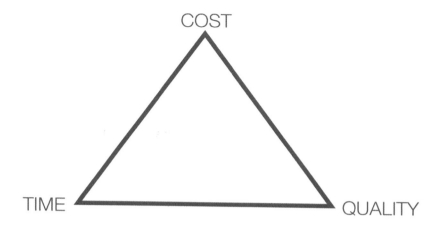

I was grateful for the lesson.

While you should never accept second best this needs to be tempered with a reality that the objectives you seek can be inter-related. What you seek in one dimension will compromise or impact on other areas.

Your final decision will be a judgement call on what key goals are achieved, and at what cost.

It can be stupid to be like an agency, expecting everything, without conceding on some things.

Principle 7: Break the rules

My youngest daughter was in a hurry, doing a quick shopping trip, where she only wanted a few things and didn't even pick up a basket, let alone a trolley.

With her shopping precariously balanced against her body she queued in the 'six items or less' line at the checkouts. The rest of the checkouts had long queues of shopping trolleys filled to their brims.

To her horror, as it became her turn to be served, she realised she actually had seven items and was about to abandon her position in the queue.

I remonstrated with her to stay in the queue. In my opinion she was not compromising the spirit of the rule, just the precise detail, which any reasonable person witnessing her predicament would not feel aggrieved. (She could have also created some added value by politely asking the people around her would they mind if she stayed in the queue.)

Is it the spirit or the detail of rules which is important in our society?

You might say, what if everything took to defining rules in what suited them, would we not have anarchy?

Firstly, there are laws and laws. A law ensuring you do not cause causing physical harm to other people, or respect their property is somewhat different from a guideline to ensure smooth operation of supermarket queues.

Our society functions because of reciprocal altruism – where it is in our vested interest to do, and be good. That's why you let other cars out in a busy road, because one day it could be you waiting in the side road.

We all the break the 'rules' – whether it is going beyond the call of duty in your own life, through to being nice to other people, (is there an unwritten law that says you cannot be nice!)

The guiding rule, I would suggest, is to obey key principles and not compromise the interests of reciprocal altruism. Do what you would have done unto yourself.

Life is about making judgment calls – including laws and how you respond to them.

What 'rules' are you cowed by? What 'prisons' have you created in your own mind about what you can, or cannot do?

Some of your best ideas will actually grow from situations where things have gone wrong, or what television's 'Blackadder' would describe as *a visit from Captain Cock-up*.

Something not going to plan, or being seen as a knock-back, a negative can often be one of the best friends to your creativity. The posh word for this is 'disruptive thinking'. It gets you thinking from a different place, it's different box thinking.

Sometimes, you also need to remember that meander is sometimes the best route. It is after all how nature operates. Rivers don't follow straight lines, but lines of least resistance.

Where are the lines of least resistance in your life when confronting stupidity?

(And remember these 'laws' are made to be broken.)

Principle 7 and a half: Great changes can be made by lots of little steps

In my talks I get two members of the audience to take part in a demonstration. I ask the more athletic of the two to leap as far as possible in one bound with both feet together. Before asking the other to make a similar leap I change the instructions to go forward instead by placing one foot in front of the other and keep going.

Guess who travels the furthest? The person with one mighty stride or the multitude of small steps? The theatre of the exercise wonderfully demonstrates the value of many small changes, perhaps reflecting how nature works, where dramatic outcomes come from a multitude of incremental changes, rather than the one big change, the one big idea.

It also symbolises that not every idea is an instant solution. Every idea represents a stepping stone in your journey of discovery of the new.

Most of your initial ideas will inevitably be of poor quality. I call these 'ideapoo'. To be outstanding in creativity you need to develop a tolerance of ideapoo. At the outset you do not know if there any real gems of ideas are hidden with your ideapoo.

You can make a small step now to tackle stupidity. What other small steps can you add? Keep going ...

Tools to help your flexible thinking

Using the key principles to empower you to stand up to stupidity around you, the next challenge is how you can make the most of the flexible thinking toolbox already in your head.

Your skills will be expanded and used more effectively if you understand how your creative thinking works and how ideas are passed on from one person to another.

Tool #1 How using your different thinking quotients can make you effectively bovvered to tackle stupidity?

The key to outstanding flexible thinking is being able to mix the right cocktail. The ingredients are your different thinking quotients.

We have an Intelligence Quotient (IQ) which features our logical, analytical fear of failure thoughts. I call these your Red Light thinking skills.

We also have an Emotional Quotient (EQ) containing your imaginative, intuitive, vision of success ideas characterised by our ability to empathise and understand other people's emotions. I call these your Green Light thinking skills

When faced with a problem an effective script for creative thinking is to initially use your Red Light thinking to analyse and identify the assumptions you or other people are making. This will assess whether, if you continue doing what you are doing, you will get the results you want and define your beautiful questions.

If you do need to generate new solutions your Green Light thinking can generate new alternatives, new questions and challenges to your assumptions.

Following on from your Green Light thinking you then need to revisit your Red Light Thinking to logically assess which of your new ideas adds most value and map out the logistics of how to make your ideas happen.

But none of this thinking will go anywhere unless you have a Vision Quotient to give a direction, a way forward for your ideas. A vision acts in giving you a sense of where you are going with your ideas. It is the picture in your head of what you want to achieve.

A strong, coherent vision also acts as a magnet in attracting you towards it. The more you can clearly see, feel, articulate your vision, the more potent a tool it becomes to making your dream a reality – whether it is a creative idea or overcoming someone else's stupidity

Added to these three quotients is the most fundamental of all your resources, your AQ, your Adversity Quotient.

Now matter how strong and potent your vision you will inevitably run into obstacles, potential barriers that prevent you from reaching where you want to be. The greatest challenge of the anti-stupidity activist is not to give in.

Adversity quotient is the will to succeed, your resilience, the ability to bounce back, not be deterred in your quest.

In order to do anything, our task must have meaning. Many people have a wishbone for their backbone. Backbone, your Adversity Quotient, is your rocket fuel to power you in your quest to tackle stupidity.

The challenge in harnessing your creative, flexible thinking is that there is no one consistent recipe of the balance between your different thinking quotients.

Sometimes you may need lots of Vision Quotient to provide a way ahead where others are limited by their blindness. In other situations there may already be too much vision, too much dreaming and the optimum added value solution is just to knuckle down and get things done.

Similarly, there will be occasions when there needs to be an emphasis on analysis where your Red Light thinking should dominate, while in other times there may be a paralysis by analysis and you need fresh new ideas created by your Green Light Thinking.

Yes, you will need Adversity Quotient to overcome, but there are times when you could be over adversarial and too much AQ could be counter-productive.

Do you just wish the world was not so stupid? Or do you want to do something about it? Check the ingredients of your cocktail of thinking quotients and check how relevant they are to your challenge.

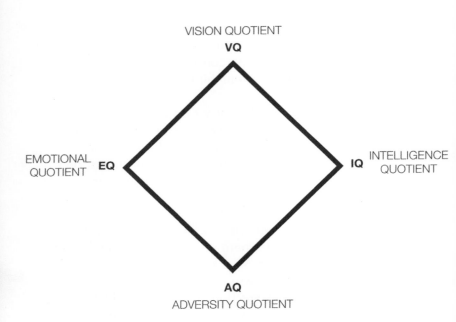

Tool # 2 By using your different attitude states you can listen with arrogance

You need arrogance, a self belief, to succeed. Yet you need to temper your arrogance with humility; a recognition that you do not know everything and are willing to listen and learn even from the most unlikely of sources. It means you are on the lookout for the new.

Arrogance without humility is hubris – false pride almost inevitably preceding a fall.

At the other extreme you can be a 'victim' characterised by a permanent and pervasive pessimism; whatever you do you tell yourself you will not succeed, and your vision is permanently set in the negative that you never have succeeded in the past, nor will you in the future. There are people sadly, in our world who have a victim mindset to seemingly everything in their lives.

Each of us has silos of 'victim' thinking. I am reckoned to startle people with my optimism yet when it comes to my weighing less I am a victim. Somehow I feel it is beyond my power and capability to be the weight level of the personal brand I want to be.

The ideal attitude state for generating new ideas, being flexible and tackling stupidity needs to combine the arrogance qualities of 'hubris' – you need a positive sense of self belief about your ability to come up with a solution, and that it is your responsibility to do something, coupled with humility that good can come from the most unlikely or unexpected of sources.

Hence, I believe I am right (using my positive arrogance) and it is my responsibility to create a new word, 'Hibris' – a positive belief in your own capabilities tempered with knowing you don't know it all.

By having this flexible attitude state it makes you more resourceful and adaptable when facing the challenge of overcoming stupidity.

Tool # 3 How using your different thinking boxes you can go large, small, or somewhere different.

You have probably heard the phrase 'outside the box thinking', often used to describe an idea, thought, or way of doing that is completely or significantly different to what has gone before.

To demonstrate how we think in boxes try this simple exercise with a group of friends.

Without conferring, write down the first five words each of you associate with the following words:

    Train   *Coffee*   *Paper*

Compare how many of the words do you have exactly the same. (If you do have the same words check if they are in the same order, written in capitals or lower case, or if there are any other differences.) I have done this exercise with hundreds of groups in my creativity sessions. With groups of three or four people not one group will have the same five words.

The reason you each use different words, even with apparently relatively simple concepts such as 'train', 'coffee', and 'paper' is because you perceive the world, every object within it, uniquely through a picture frame shaped by your values, beliefs, experiences and connections. This picture frame is called a 'frame' or a paradigm. Or I would call it a 'box'.

I would suggest that there is no such thing as 'outside the box thinking' as all ideas are within 'boxes' – as revealed in my encounter with the florist (on pages 34-5); she had a narrow definition of her job role. I had a bigger definition of her service role, but was equally guilty of narrowly defining the opportunity before me of getting a rose to my wife, which blinded me to the wider opportunity of not making wider use of a full bouquet of flowers I was paying for.

Our thinking has the option to flexibly jump between same box, smaller box, bigger box or different box thinking. (In the examples below I am using the imaginary potential responses of the waitress who wouldn't slice a lemon for my drink, to show how these different thinking boxes operate.)

Same box thinking – you think and do what everyone else is doing and what is expected of you. (Waitress: *My boss told me not to slice the lemon. So, I won't.*)

Bigger box thinking – you go beyond on a bigger scale, or in new dimensions to explore new elements to add to your mix or make new connections between previously unrelated items. (Waitress: *I will raise this problem about slicing lemons with the company and get it to review and hopefully change its policies.*)

Smaller box thinking – you change a part of the whole, using an element or niche to create new interest or opportunities. (Waitress: *This is just a one-off, special request, so I will slice the lemon for this customer.*)

Different box thinking – you start from somewhere different, often prompted by a provocation such as a creativity technique or even an operational occurrence (cock up). (Waitress: *Maybe, I could go to the bar next door and get a lemon for this customer.*)

<u>One of the most powerful creativity tools at your disposal</u> – it is a simple question. The question is: *'What assumptions are we making here?'*

By posing this question it unravels the assumptions you, your colleagues, your boss, your marketplace or the world at large is making, and identifies the boxes surrounding their thinking.

By understanding you have four different thinking strategies this puts you at an advantage over those limited to same box thinking.

By adopting the principles of both a helicopter and microscopic view, above, beyond and within the situation, it gives you greater flexibility in your thinking. This use of different degrees of observing a situation gives you the ability to step back quicker to go forward faster when confronting and tackling any problem.

Tool # 4 How using your sagacity will help you spot opportunities others will miss.

We are all never more than 12ft from an opportunity. (In one week I came across two statistics: in a building you are never more than 12ft from an electric motor, or a rat!) Believing in synchronicity, the same must apply to ideas.

The Millennium footbridge across the River Thames was closed within three days after its opening in June 2000 because it had a 'wobble'. (I met someone who was among the visitors on its opening who told me how complete strangers were coming together to do spontaneous group duck walks!)

The wobble, or to give the phenomena its proper title, 'synchronous lateral excitation', was caused by pedestrians unconsciously adjusting their pace to walk in step with the minute vibrations given off by the footbridge when it was being used by a large number of people.

In fairness to the engineers, since few footbridges in the world had previously accommodated such large numbers as the Millennium Bridge, the phenomenon was relatively unknown and could not have been easily predicted.

The problem of the wobble was however, self-limiting. Beyond a certain point, it simply becomes impossible to get any more people on the bridge. As it gets fuller, people stop moving and the effect subsides, long before structural safety limits are reached.

The decision was taken to 'repair' the bridge and eliminate the wobble. Some £5 million of repairs later the bridge was reopened in February 2002.

The 'wobble' was not part of the engineering spec. But was the wobble a problem?

Imagine you are in the Mayor of an ordinary mediaeval Italian town.

Through one office door enters your chief engineer: *"Boss, we gotta problem with our bell tower. It's developed a lean! We need to spend five million lire to put it straight."*

Your head of tourism disagrees: *"There might be something in this."* Who should you listen to?

The Millennium footbridge is not just a means of helping people to get across the river. It is also a tourist attraction. The wobble, like the lean in the tower of Pisa was an opportunity. Tourists would have gone out of their way to visit 'the wobbly bridge'.

Instead, costly alterations were made, and the scheme came in over budget and delayed, undermining the reputation of British engineering of an otherwise elegant and stylish structure.

Opportunities are all around you. The challenge is they are often camouflaged, half concealed, inverted, not overt.

By believing in opportunities and seeing the bigger picture – your sagacity – can help you spot them and use them to overcome stupidity.

Tool # 5 How using different thinking spectacles can help you see the creative potential of yourself, and other people.

There is no such thing as a creative and non-creative person. The creative task has many different facets requiring specific talents at different stages to fully realize the potential of an idea. Creativity spans the origination, nurturing and realization of an idea. We all have differing strengths and weaknesses for the different aspects of creativity.

Who is more creative? The person who is articulate and lucid in generating many ideas quickly, who shines at brainstorms? Or the person who might actually says less, but the ideas they do proffer are generally better formed and worked out and are of a higher quality? Or what about the person who may be weak on the initial sparking of ideas, but is better at realizing the idea, overcoming the barriers and obstacles to make it happen?

We each see the world uniquely through different paradigms or boxes. We also have what I call creative thinking spectacles, which frame and focus how we view the world and shapes our response. (Organizations can also be characterized by having a dominant style of creative thinking spectacles.)

The good news is that there is no right or wrong creative thinking spectacle. Each has its merits. They also have their own disadvantages. Here are four categories to label the different spectacle types.

Directors
Possess extremely clear focus, able to quickly define with
great clarity what they see as the 'problem' or 'solution'
and move quickly and decisively in dealing with their
'problem'. They tend to be highly driven, wanting to be
decisive and take control.

They may however, be too narrowly focused, blind to
other options or opportunities, which could have yielded
far greater added value.

Enthusiasts
With their high levels of energy they view a world
of infinite variety and complexity with a playfulness,
contorting, combining, or adapting the different elements
before them.

By being alert to a world of rich variety, they may
however overlook the obvious or the clear-cut, and then
over-elaborate, and not do the simple or obvious.

Analysts
Examining a world of detailed order, structure and logical
process before them, this helps them organize their
thoughts and realities. They are however, uncomfortable
when it doesn't go to plan and sometimes the plan can
become an end in itself rather than a tool.

Team players
See a world sensitive to emotional undercurrents and
its inter-connected network of personal relationships. In
seeing the rich emotional dimension they can shy away
from tackling problems and instinctively seek consensus
as a solution.

By understanding your own creative thinking spectacle style you can pay to your strengths and also appreciate your potential limitations.

By recognising the creative thinking style of others, whether it is a person or an organization, you can better understand how they are thinking and how to best respond to their way of thinking.

To a Director you emphasise options and results. They want to be in control and make choices.

An Enthusiast will entertain further variety and options to consider.

Analysts want facts, logic and a proper procedure to go forward with.

Team players want balance, harmony, and goodwill where conflict and decisions are avoided where possible.

The challenge is to recognise and respect the different profiles, and identify how to flexibly respond to them. By doing so, you can improve your chances of overcoming the other person's stupidity by tailoring your message to their type of creative thinking spectacles.

Your toolbox

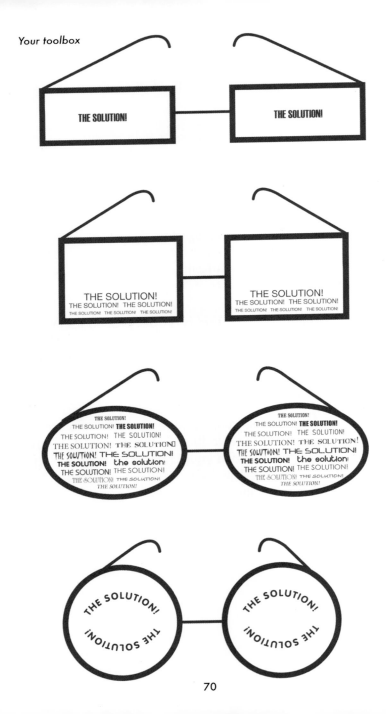

Part Three

(or Part 1 if you are reading in reverse order!)

Taking on Stupidity

Armed with your understanding of stupidity along with an appreciation of your own mental toolbox of flexible thinking skills, you are now better equipped to take on stupidity.

What key principles can you now use? How is your reality like that of an Australian in the equatorial rain forest? What specific responses can you use to the different situations you face?

Sam's Law

I had the pleasure of touring Australia giving talks and supporting the work of the nation's creative industries sector.

While in Brisbane I met Sam Nicolosi, who ran the Queensland Creative Industries Skills Council. In his spare time Sam was also a volunteer park ranger in the Equatorial Rain Forest Park on the outskirts of the city.

Sam kindly took me on a fascinating tour of the Park. Telling Sam how lucky he was to have this dimension in his life, his response was *"Well, most of the time."* When pressed about his uncertain response, he told me how he was irritated when the Park authorities cancelled his tours when it rained.

If I had been a branding consultant about the time the world was created I would have been proud of 'Equatorial Rain Forest'. It inherently contains the it-does-what-it-says-on-the-tin qualities of: it's in an equatorial area, it has trees, and it ... erm, rains there. Sam's disappointment was not focussed on the inconvenience he suffered. Rather it denied visitors the opportunity to witness the rain forest in all its glory; the vegetation would demonstrate nature's wonderful architecture for the heavy rainfall, with magnificent sights of the plant's rain channels and the cascades they created....

Innocently, on asking why they cancelled the tours when it rains I was told, it was a precautionary measure in case anyone slipped.

"Had anyone slipped when on a tour of the Park in the rain?" I enquired of Sam. *"No"* was his reply.

As I had such a great time on my tour with Sam I thought I would repay the kindness and hospitality by devising what I would call 'Sam's Law' – six rules to provide him with ammunition to deal with the bureaucrats in his life; it is also a useful response for anyone having to deal with the bureaucrats and stupidity in your life.

Rule #1 Mr. or Mrs Bureaucrat stop being so creative!

During my Stupid Aid tour of 2007 I was interviewed by BBC Radio Newcastle about stupidity in the world and turning the tables on them I asked them of any examples they had come across.

They shared a story about a table. During a major campaign to encourage bird watching they wanted to put up a bird table in their car park only to be refused permission on grounds of health and safety; the bird table might fall on someone!

I then asked: *"Has a bird table fallen on anyone in the BBC Radio Newcastle car park?"* The situation was seemingly without precedent.

The story demonstrates how people who say 'No' are actually demonstrating great, original creative thought, albeit in a negative mode.

In my creativity talks I pose a question: Anyone here got the equivalent of a first class honours degree at Cambridge University in *'Future visualization – the ability to create new, imaginary futures'*? (The essence of Green Light Thinking) On getting nil response I reframe the question: *"Anyone here good at worrying?"*

I get an overwhelming 'Yes' response. (If there was such a degree at Cambridge University, everyone is confident they would you get a first class honours degree.)

If you are brilliant at worrying, you are equally brilliant at creativity.

Yet what is the difference worrying and being creative? Both work on the mechanics of having a small piece of information and then creating a false imaginary image of a possible future.

In my Stupid Aid talks I get the audience to hold a sheet a paper and with their eyes shut follow a set of instructions of folding and tearing specific corners off the sheet. Invariably, few will have a resulting sheet looking like mine. At different stages of the instructions there is scope for slight variables to creep into the process leading to many different outcomes.

So when a bureaucrat predicts an outcome they are actually using future visualization and being creative by devising one (and only one) imaginary future scenario, or transferring an experience in one area and applying it in a new, novel context.

Just like the paper tearing exercise, there is no certainty that only one predicted outcome will materialise. Their scenario is potentially one among an infinite number of potential futures.

We do face the certainty that if anyone actively looks for a potential problem, they can invariably always find one. As my mate Trevor says: *"A blind squirrel will always find a nut."*

So Rule # 1 of Sam's Law is to ask has the worst case scenario ever happened. Alternatively, has the best case scenario been envisaged with as much vigour?

Had anyone slipped over on a rainforest walk? Was the splendour of a rainstorm experience in the forest fully realised before it was rejected?

Isn't it great that even the most stubborn of bureaucrats is actually revealing their inherent creative talent for devising new scenarios or transferring ideas from one context to another?

Rule #2 What little medicine can be taken?

People with ideas can be keen, enthusiastic, and posses an abundant energy to realise their potential. They can also be metaphorically blind and deaf.

Sometimes you can be too precious about protecting your idea. So when one person says 'No' you may get ultra defensive and be blind or deaf to the reality of what the other person is actually saying to you. You could be missing out some valid feedback which, if you took on board, would make your idea more robust and more powerful.

Whenever anyone says 'No' explore if there is any little medicine which can be added to your idea which could overcome the objection. There is a tendency to totally accept or reject ideas. By using your small box thinking it might be possible to identify suitable antidotes to the objection.

In the example of BBC Radio Newcastle some efforts could have been made to make any bird table in the car park ultra safe with some design modifications. You should always be prepared to dance with bureaucrats to help both of you change your positions.

For Sam and his tours of the equatorial rain forest it might consist of advising of the potential risk of slippage, insisting walkers wear suitable footwear, and maybe adding extra safety elements such as handrails at vulnerable parts of the trail.

Rule #3 What bigger picture is revealed by objection?

Is the problem or objection to your idea part of a wider issue or malaise? Do the questions raised reveal bigger issues?

In the example of Sam's walks being cancelled is there for example, adequate insurance cover in place?

You can often find that what might appear a petty objection can uncover genuine wider issues. The person with the idea can be deaf to potentially constructive feedback.

In assessing bigger picture issues you need to be careful of striking a balance with other parts of Sam's Law. The decision-makers, whether they are in the Equatorial Rain Forest or in a restaurant not serving lemons, were using bigger picture thinking to create a vision for the risks they perceived in banning the walks in the rain, or the slicing of lemons.

Use an objection as a cue to step back and assess the bigger implications of what you want to do. Identify how you can do things differently as a result.

Rule #4 Challenge the 'sanctity paradigm'

You can sometimes come against the equivalent of a metaphorical brick wall when faced with someone backing up their arguments with phrases such as it is, 'health and safety', 'national security', 'the war against terrorism', 'financial probity' or 'data protection'.

What these people are actually using is what is called a 'sanctity paradigm' – a platform of argument making it difficult to establish a legitimate position against, where no right-minded person would seemingly argue against these points.

The ground upon which your opponent is arguing from is effectively sanctified.

When faced with a sanctity paradigm your goal is to create an even higher level, or bigger box, of argument, where you propose 'intelligent use of health and safety', 'intelligent defence of national security, or war on terrorism', 'intelligent use of financial controls' or 'intelligent use of data protection'.

An alternative strategy in dealing with a 'sanctity paradigm' is to use small box thinking and explore a small part, a detail rather than meet their line of argument head-on. If for example, someone raised an objection because of 'data protection' respond by asking: *'What aspect of data protection is contravened?'*

Rule #5 Can you be magnificent?

Problems don't always have to be bad news.

If you can anticipate a negative scenario you can also identify how you can be magnificent in responding to the problem, to turn a complainer into an advocate.

You can relate to the example of complaining in a restaurant, for the complaint to be handled in a way that delights you.

Sure, problems may materialise, but ask a beautiful question: *'What ways can you be magnificent?'*

The problem could be transformed into a wonderful opportunity. (How about a lemon slicing franchise in every restaurant!)

Rule #6 What would your role model do?

In the world of great complexity. It can be like a fog of uncertainty. What do you do, what is the right thing to do?

In these situations a brilliant technique is to use role models – people or things that can inspire you. It can be someone you may know, or famous, or dead or alive, fact or fiction. I even had one delegate suggest their cat. (Who, by the way, was called Stan).

One of my favourite roles models is the lieutenant character played by Tom Hanks in the film *'Saving Private Ryan'*. In the film he embodied good sense, decency and resourcefulness: 'What would he do if faced with a problem?'

What would he do if he worked at BBC Newcastle and faced the request for a bird table to be put in the car park? Or if he was a park manager in the equatorial rain forest, or in charge of slicing lemons at a restaurant chain?

What would he do with the next example of stupidity you will encounter?

Top 30 hit parade of common examples of stupid thinking

Armed with your key principles, range of flexible thinking tools and Sam's Law you now have a more extensive toolbox to challenge stupidity wherever you come across it.

Here are some frequently found examples of stupid responses you may encounter, and some suggested responses.

Example # 1 *'This is the thin end of the wedge – it will set a precedent'*

Precedent is only a legitimate issue in a court of law. (And even then a judge may recognize a change in context to apply a new interpretation.)

Committing yourself to a decision does not mean that act or response is now set in stone for any future situation. It is not a legal precedent. It is merely a response to a specific, given situation.

No one steps in the same river twice. The context of any act will always be different, unique in space and time.

Faced with any new situation you should be pragmatic and flexible, judging every situation on its merits.

Unless of course you're a judge in a court of law, where you do actually set precedent. Are you a mighty judge in wig and robes? Or are you someone making pragmatic decisions in your world?

Example # 2 *'The computer says 'No' (or ,'sorry it's our rules')*

Rules are never set in stone. They were made by someone. Get them to adapt, be flexible, or change them.

It is patent nonsense for anyone to say the operating rules of their business cannot be changed.

Be persistent. Highlight the idiocy of blindly obeying an instruction.

Someone, somewhere is in charge of the computer.

Get hold of them and get them to do something about it.

Ask to speak to the manager, and if necessary, their manager. Go to the top. (A good tip for getting the extension number of the most senior manager in an organization is to ask for the extension number of their PA and then try the numbers either side of that.)

The computer system is a tool, not a master.

Remember, *'Orders from above'* has a nasty historical echo to it.

Example # 3 *'It's been approved by experts'*

Experts can get it wrong.

'Experts' once thought the world was flat.

Are they appropriate experts?

Are there other experts whose expertise is greater or more relevant?

Some great challenging questions when faced with stupidity are:

Who says?

So what?

Why not?

What evidence have you got?

What is the size of their sample from which they are drawing conclusions?

Example #4 *'There is no precedent for this'*

Create a precedent. Do something new.

Just because something has not evidently happened before, it doesn't mean it should never happen.

Was there a precedent for the computer, antibiotics, or cheesy quaver crisps? Just think if we had said: 'No we can't use these ideas as there is no precedent.'

If we all think like this we will never have any progress.

Example #5 *'We've already spent so much on this, we should continue'*

What is past is gone and you can't get back what you spent in time, money, or emotion.

Your decision making is set in the now. It is about managing and securing the best future for you.

Your judgment should be based on what is the best outcome, not the best justification on what has been spent before.

Example #6 *'This proves my point'*

Are you just looking for confirmation of your existing point of view?

We cocoon ourselves with information that substantiates our world view. Are there other points that have been overlooked and not taken into account? Or has the value of other information been judged in a skewed way?

In researching for this book I was going to include the story about John F. Kennedy where he apparently inadvertently declared: *'He was a jelly donut'* to a Berlin audience. (The gaffe is evidently caused by 'Berliner' also meaning a type of donut.)

Yet, his audience knew precisely what Kennedy meant to say. There was no contemporary comment about a perceived gaffe.

The urban legend grew, presumably out of a desire to debunk a famous political figure, perhaps with a dose of anti-American sentiment thrown in, along with its humour value as a funny story. By passing on the information the teller is improving their self esteem and status, either as someone who knows funny tales or has some historical or political insight.

Always double-check the evidence. Is the story you hear, the real story, or the story you want to hear?

Are you guilty of prejudice or stereotyping? What seemingly validates your point of view could actually lead to compound stupidity.

Example #7 *'It's easy'*

What is your confidence based on?

Overconfidence, whether you're a driver, doctor, or designer of space shuttles can lead to fatal consequences. Most people regard themselves as above average when it comes to judging their own abilities.

Positive confidence is a crucial ingredient of hibris, in believing you can be successful.

Overconfidence however, can lead to hubris where you don't appreciate, or fail to work on your weaknesses as much as you should.

Some things are easy. And stupidity is one of them.

Example #8 *'I'm proud of that'*

Sometimes it's hard to throw away something you have owned whether it is an item in your garage that hasn't been used for some time, or a body of ideas and opinions that you have not challenged over the years.

You tend to put a personal value on something far greater than it should merit, if it has been part of you for some time. This can lead to distortion and inappropriate values being placed on something, leading to stupidity.

Celebrate your pride, recognise its value to your past, but don't let it solely define your present or future.

Pride can lead to vanity – and stupidity.

Example #9 *'It's a problem, so needs sorting'*

What is the price of the solution? Does it outweigh the benefits?

A road under a bridge in my home town floods maybe once or twice a year, making it impassable for a day or two.

So, for one or two days a year the road is blocked. It is now being solved with a repair scheme that will eliminate the problem. Yippee!

The repair will however, result in the road being out of action for 18 months – the equivalent to 540 days or 270 years of the current level of inconvenience.

Wouldn't it be better to just accept the problem and live a life around it, rather than solving, at a Pyrrhic cost, where the pain of the solution far outweighs its benefits?

Sometimes solutions can be more stupid than the problems they are solving.

Example #10 *'I was just reading about how parachuting is dangerous, and what about these terrorists?'*

Just because something is reported in the news it doesn't mean it will happen to you.

Despite the focus that terrorism has received in recent years, the risk of dying from terrorism is very low compared to much more mundane ways to die such as driving off the road (80 times more likely to kill you) or even a hernia (5 times more likely to kill you). *

Misleading vividness can lead you to make stupid assumptions. Always take a breath and assess the real, likely impact, rather than what's front of mind from the front page you have been reading.

It's easy to overestimate the significance or likelihood of something which is in the front of your mind, and overlook or underestimate the significance of less prominent things.

In your daily schedule how much are you bogged down by what is urgent rather than what is important.

Much stupidity in terms of our prioritizing and use of our precious resources can be caused by responding to the urgent, rather than asking a beautiful question of 'what is important?'

(*article in *Wired.com* by Ryan Singel.)

Example #11 *'They are acting like a stupid idiot'*

Is the other driver who cuts you up on the road a stupid idiot, or worse?

Or are they a good, kind person who may have just been momentarily distracted by something else in their life?

Most people tend to exaggerate other people's personality attributes into good or bad.

The writer Kurt Vonnegut coined the term 'granfalloons' to describe 'proud and meaningless associations of human beings'. What do you think of Adolf Hitler, Joseph Stalin or Osama Bin Laden? You might hold them in higher esteem if your birthday is on April 20th, December 21st, or March 10th – their respective birthdays.

Even sharing a birthday with someone can influence how they are seen.

What is distorting your view – either as a halo effect, (or the opposite, the horn effect) in judging other people's actions?

Are they really stupid, or is your response to them stupid?

As my friend Geoff Roberts reminds me, how about going round with a belief *'they are doing their best'* – after all, you are, aren't you? This can be difficult; you do not know what is going on in their life possibly distracting them, or making them less effective. They will always be doing their best for themselves – we are all, ultimately, selfish.

Example #12 *"Shut happens' - it might provoke a complaint so we don't do it'*

In the same way a blind squirrel will always find a nut, so bureaucrats can find excuses for saying 'No' by using their creative talent to conjure up the prospect of an imaginary person making a complaint.

Rejecting new ideas on the basis that someone might complain is an excuse to settle for the mediocrity, the bland and the lowest common denominator.

I was running a creativity session for a museum service. One problem raised was how the museum frequently closes one of its galleries for exhibition changeovers which irritated visitors.

One partial remedy we created, on the principle of always turning negatives into positives, was to make the closure signs humorous in some ways. I had earlier spotted a shop with a closed sign saying: *'Shut happens'.* *"Why couldn't we use that?"* I suggested. *"Oh no, we couldn't possibly."* The museum staff replied. *"The head of services won't let us. She would say it would get a complaint."*

So the idea was stillborn.

Has the complaint been made? How significant is the complainer? For every complainer how many more people would actually benefit? What other forms of feedback should be recognized? What about the positives the idea could create?

How many other organizations similarly stifle creativity, the chance to add value to the performance, service or experience? It's stifled by someone saying 'No' about an imaginary scenario that could just as well not happen as happen.

The comedian Kenny Everett had a great sketch about the BBC bureaucrat whose office door brass plaque declared: *'Man in charge of saying 'No'*. If you say 'No' you are sadly, less likely to be made accountable for the cost of your intransigence.

I remember a story about a major advertising agency being hauled in by its client who had received a complaint about its latest campaign. The 'complaint' turned out to be just one letter from a member of the public. The client unused to this visible type of feedback, over-reacted. Soon afterwards the agency encouraged a friend to write to the client company praising the ad. The issue -where there were an equal number of letters in support and against the campaign - was amazingly nullified in the client's mind.

Nearly every cherished icon of creativity was either rejected at the outset, or faced complaints. New Yorkers initially couldn't be bothered to raise the money for the plinth for the Statue of Liberty, even though they were getting the statue free as a gift from France.

Remember Sam's Law and challenge and complain about the bureaucrats.

Example #13 *'We have always done it this way. It worked last time.'*

In a faster moving world, solutions which worked in one situation will increasingly be less reliable for new challenges because the context will be different in some way.

You also need to account for significant shifts which can impact on you.

Imagine you are a turkey. You look back on your previous life as one characterized by being regularly fed, gaining weight and all in life is good. Will that necessarily be the case next week, or the week after?

The only way to cope with the immensity of managing a fast moving environment, or the possibility of profound shifts in your environment, is through harnessing your creative, flexible thinking.

Example #14 *'This was the first thing that came to hand'*

Doing the first, the easy, or seemingly obvious thing is not always the best response.

Have you played that silly childish game of asking people for an immediate answer to a question posed after endlessly repeating the word *'Silk'*? Most people will invariably answer the question 'What do cows drink?' replying with *'Milk'* (Actually, in small box thinking term, baby cows do drink milk!)

If something is commonplace then it is often likely to be the solution which is easiest rather than best.

If the value of a solution to your problem is low, then go with the easy. If not, use you flexible thinking skills of bigger, smaller or different box thinking to come up with new alternatives.

Example #15 *'I wasn't asked the right question?'*

The quality of how you interact with the world around is through the quality of your questions.

Recognise how there is always more than one question, and the significance of questions can be determined by their context. The more beautiful your question, the more beautiful the potential outcome.

Context determines the significance of something. Your questions shape how you perceive the context of any challenge facing you.

A recent GCSE Religious Education exam had a question: *'What is God?'* [2 marks]

What questions are you waiting to be asked? Have they got the right score?

Example #16 *'I'll try and sort it out?'*

Do this exercise. Stand behind a chair. Pick the chair up. OK you accomplished that task. Now, don't pick the chair up. That was probably even easier to do.

Now, try to pick the chair up. Try to ...

At this moment if your doing the exercise I can envisage you're uncertain about what exactly you can do to achieve the task.

How can you 'try' to pick something up? In life, you can either do it, or not do it. There's no half-way house. If you say you will try to get something done. It won't get done.

Saying you will 'try to do something' is a stupid response in a faster moving world, where you will need clarity of understanding about what will, and what will not get done.

Stupidity is very trying. Trying is stupid.

Example #17 *'I believe I'm stupid'*

That's a really helpful response. Why don't you just cop out, and run away from your responsibilities to face the challenges in your life?

Whether it is believing you are not creative, or are stupid, self-handicapping yourself with these sorts of statements and beliefs can act as a self-fulfilling promise.

The good news is you can actually change your beliefs.

How many adult Christians believe in Father Christmas? Considerably more believed in him when they were younger. This is a demonstration of how people can change their beliefs.

A good tool to assist changing your beliefs is to give your goal - such as changing your belief you are stupid - added significance or meaning. You can do this by linking it with something you know is important to you. Your thought processes could go along the lines of: *'I really want to get on in my career. So it is important I manage this issue of stupidity around me by believing I am creative (not stupid).'*

Alternatively, use the opposite strategy of diluting the significance of the negative belief, such as believing you are stupid in a wider context: *'These things that make me look stupid are not as important as other things in my life.'*

Example #18 *'I know what to expect, I have already made up my mind'*

Writing the script for a future encounter in your life can be helpful. But remember plans are useless but planning is essential.

Even the most thorough of plans needs to be tempered with flexibility. You need to have a hibris attitude state where you recognize you don't know everything and are willing to take new things on from the unlikeliest of sources. Otherwise, you could be intransigent, blind to new challenges or opportunities.

Never set your expectations in stone.

Check what stereotypes or prejudices you are using.

There is usually always scope for change. Always be open to giving a second chance.

You future script could have a happier ending.

Example #19 *'I saw it with my own eyes'*

Sometimes things seen first hand will be seen as more valid than something more abstract, although potentially more valid.

Your eyes and ears are valuable tools. Always harness your eyes and ears as opportunity spotting tools.

Encounters with other people are often taken over by the desire to impress the other person rather than you wanting to be changed by what they have to say. (The old advice that your ears will never get you into trouble is so true.)

You do however, owe it to your most precious tool, your mind, to supply it with information from the widest of sources before you make any judgement.

Do not let the way you obtained the information distort your evaluation.

Example #20 *'It's not logical therefore cannot be considered'*

Things do not always go in logical steps along one line.

Nature doesn't work like that, where progress is many small steps, but the slightest distortion can lead to profound differences from the original path.

Life rarely follows an exact, sequential process of one thing indeterminably leading to another. Rivers meander, following lines of least resistance.

Your intuitive skills are just as important as your rational logical thoughts. Many of the most important decisions in your life, such as choosing your life partner, are not based on logic.

Learn to listen to your intuition and trust its judgement, so long as it is not based on fear. Check you are asking your intuition the right questions.

Reflecting back on every bad decision I have made in my life, invariably, with hindsight, there were warning signs, alerts that I should have spotted, yet failed to.

I remember when my first business partner did the dirty on me, and my wife reflected: *"I knew we shouldn't have trusted her after she served tin carrots for dinner!"*

Listen to your intuition. Life is not logical. Remember to harness your Green Light thinking skills. Sometimes stupidity can be at the end of a logical conclusion.

Example #21 *'Something might turn up!'*

Waiting for something good, the wishful feeling that your blind positive optimism will be rewarded can give you a nice warm feeling.

Sometimes delaying a decision might indeed be the best option.

Sometimes however, something might not turn up.

One really good tool I use for making a decision is to toss a coin. Heads I do it, tails I don't. But rather than rest my decision on the fate of the coin, I actually use the coin's toss to trigger my intuitive thoughts.

Should the coin land heads for a 'yes' decision, I listen within for any feeling, urge or voice encouraging me to toss the coin again. This is my intuition telling me it's either the wrong decision, or the wrong time to make a decision.

Procrastination however, can also be an excuse for avoiding uncomfortable issues or decisions, which if left unchecked will only get worse. What is the cost or penalty from not making a decision?

You may tend to over-estimate the possibility of desired, positive things over undesired, negative possibilities.

It can be stupid waiting for a knight in shining armour, or for a prince, or princess, to kiss your frog, while problems build up around you.

Example #22 *'I'm in control'*

The illusion of being in control can lead you to over-estimate how much you can actually dictate the course of events.

You can end up underestimating others things which could be as important such as luck, the general economic climate, or the decisions of a more powerful decision-maker.

It is amazing how little we can actually control: Not your breathing, your partner's spending, nor the next five minutes.

A certain legend about King Canute - when he tried, and failed, to hold back the tide – serves as a reminder that even the most powerful of people have their limitations.

PS. You can always seek to outmaneuver someone who is opposing you by asking to go to their boss, or their boss's boss.

Example #23 *'It's OK we have got lots of people supporting this'*

The mass of people don't always get it right. I take a lot of comfort from Frank Zappa's defiant statement: *"Just because several million people think I'm wrong doesn't mean they are right."*

Problems are more likely to be solved if they have a champion who has strong adversity quotient, who believes in the idea, or cause they are supporting. As a result they won't give in, or take damaging short-cuts.

Having lots of people supporting an idea is all very good. But who is at the heart of any new idea you are considering? How sufficiently motivated are they in making something happen?

Judging the motivation can be just as important as the logic and coherence of an argument. The obverse is that just because someone is committed doesn't mean their argument is similarly strong.

Look beyond the words and rationality of any stupidity. Assess how much it is being driven either by the motivation of the people behind it, or how much the majority view is because of inertia or apathy.

Is one person's stupidity driving the many? Is many people's stupidity driving you?

Example #24 *'Maybe we should repeatedly change it to see what works?'*

Frequent chopping and changing can be a stupid option. Rather than fruitfully exploring different options or dimensions making changes can often be an excuse for clear lack of control, or a weak vision about what you are trying to achieve.

Over-changing can prevent an effective solution from being developed, as the idea's potential is nipped in the bud as a result of changes in direction.

Maybe you should change, but maybe you should stick with it, persevere and not give up at the first hurdle.

The other man's grass is not always less stupid.

Example #25 *'Sometimes it helps to live a little dangerously'*

Walking the edge can often lead to falling over the edge.

I have a theory that people don't take risks.

I once did promotional work for a spinal injury charity where we obtained case studies of patients, to be used for gaining wider understanding of their situation. One case featured a guy, immobile from the waist down after being injured in a gliding accident.

Someone had foolishly left a rope across the runway causing the glider to crash to earth. I unsubtly said: *"You're lucky to be alive"*. The man bitterly replied: *"Do you call this lucky?"*

Although going in a glider is a risky experience, he didn't envisage being in a near fatal injury, spending the rest of his life in a wheelchair.

Anyone who does a dangerous sport or stunt, such as glider flying, enters the task with the conviction they will survive. Yes, people can put themselves in risky situations, doing what to others might perceive as foolhardy, but deep down in their own minds they are resigned to their success. Hence, it is not a risk.

If the consequence of the risk is low then live dangerously, break the rules if necessary.

Recklessness can wreck. Ask yourself have you truly weighed up the positive and negative consequences of your actions.

Example #26 *'It would be impolite'*

Sometimes we hold back from doing what might be the obvious or sensible solution because we are worried about other person's feelings, how they might react.

I was recently waiting in an over-long queue at airport security. I watched with growing anxiety as the clock ticked away and faced the real prospect that I was going to miss my flight as a result of being so far back in line.

I took the initiative and politely repeated: *'I'm very sorry but my gate is closing'* as I jumped the line. I may have added a further amount of angst to those frustrated in the queue, but it did mean I caught my flight and hopefully did not preclude them from catching theirs.

So long as it is a genuine situation, handled with sincere tact, then it would be stupid to miss the flight.

You need to apply reciprocal altruism. What would you want other people to do to you in the same circumstance?

It is rude to be stupid.

Example #27 *'You shouldn't ask questions'*

Questions don't hurt. Ignorance does.

The question is the most fundamental tool for the flexible thinker.

Remember, creativity is about 'flexible thinking around beautiful questions.' Stupidity is about inflexible thinking without asking questions.

You should always ask questions. (Especially stupid ones!)

Example # 28 *'It's politically incorrect'*

Political correctness, the desire to make what you say and do conform to a prevailing orthodoxy of what is right, or wrong can lead to stupid actions. That is not to say that 'political correctness' is stupid. If you value equality of opportunity, treating people the same regardless of age, creed, disability, gender, race or sexual orientation then political correctness has been a valuable tool in creating a better society.

Just watching television shows from the 1960's and '70's where racial or national stereotyping is portrayed, demonstrates the progress our society has made on these issues.

Back in 1994 I was inadvertently responsible for the Institute of Public Relations establishing its first Equal Opportunities policy; I had organized a social event with a senior local journalist acting as quizmaster. Although in my view he had a heart of gold, he reflected some values of a previous era, as evidenced when he began a question; *"Here's one for you girls. On the QWERTY keyboard where is the letter ...'* Some members complained saying surely it must be against the Institute's policy. On checking I discovered the Institute did not then have a formal policy so I began the process of creating one.

Like any tool political correctness has to be used appropriately, as it has the risk of being blunt or used indiscriminately. It's a bit like the 17th century witch hunts where too many of us are afraid to challenge what we feel is inappropriate use of political correctness.

The word 'brainstorming' is claimed to be politically incorrect, as it may upset people with epilepsy, or those sensitive to mental health issues. The words 'thought showering' or similar, apparently, should be used instead.

'What a load of codswallop' was my initial reaction. I asked several friends who had experienced epilepsy if they were upset by the word 'brainstorming'. Their reaction was even more extreme than mine! I have since done several surveys among epilepsy campaign groups, as well as those with an interest in mental health issues. I have not found anyone with a formal policy or recommendation on using 'brainstorming' and have since taken a public stand on the issue.

So we are witnessing an urban myth, or meme (see page 17), which periodically results in well-meaning people complying with 'political correctness'.

There is no formal church of political correctness, or high order determining what is, or isn't politically correct. It's a judgment call each and every one of us has to make, and stand up for, or against.

It's stupid just because something is labeled 'politically correct' you have to agree with it or not challenge it.

Example # 29 *'We need to have rules and regulations to guard against the minority of people who will abuse the system.'*

Why punish the majority to teach the few?

What is the cost to the many against the actual cost caused by a small number of people breaking the rules?

Can the minority be better targeted or subjected to specific additional measures?

Could the system be better self-regulated?

Could you create a taboo around the behaviour rather than a formal legal punishment? (My personal crusade is against people under 6ft tall sitting in the extra leg room, emergency exit seats on aircraft!)

Yes, there will be times when rules or laws are needed to be in place to ensure fairness, justice and efficiency. There will be situations where strong, clear cut rules are necessary to uphold the non-negotiables, the fundamentals of your world.

Just because something is wrong, or inconsistent with the system, by focusing on it however, you can ignore the bigger picture.

Think about how you would like to be treated, or consider the impact of any planned regulation on reciprocal altruism. Ask what would your role model do?

Inflexible thinking, without asking questions leads to stupidity.

Example # 30 *'It's data protection or health
and safety.'*

Remember Rule #4 of Sam's Law. Respond by counter-
challenging is it *intelligent* data protection or health and
safety or is it 'Duck out data protection or health and
safety?' Are they are using lazy excuses, rather than
addressing the real issue.

You can also challenge a small detail, rather than
challenge the stupidity head on. Ask: *'What aspect of
data protection is contravened?'*

Much in our modern-day life, such as data protection
or health and safety is there to help us. What ways is it
being used in unhelpful or unwise ways?

A call to action

Shakespeare once described the world as a stage where we are all but actors.

Yet, we are all actors but blessed with responsibility to mould and shape the play in the way we want it. Stupidity is about us, as actors, failing to use the most of our thinking skills.

If you believe, life is too short, and you want to be a good ancestor, you owe it to yourself to challenge stupidity.

Keeping out of stupidity is not a gift, or result of good fortune. It is as a result of what you put into it, what you gain from your learning, self development and self-discovery.

When you come across examples of stupidity it tells you about the flexibility of thinking, current skill levels, strategies and effort being applied in a situation. Stupidity is a sign to do something different in the future if you want to succeed and make the world better.

Whether you are a Stupid Aid ambassador, or just want to make your bit of the world a better place, remember to:

1. Challenge stupid bureaucracy. Make people and their organizations accountable. Stand up if you think something is wrong. Do the right thing. But remember to choose your battles.

2. Challenge lazy thinking. Don't be fobbed off with 'duck out data protection' or whatever excuse from you or other people.

3. Don't be a stupid adult – young people often don't need a good talking to, but a good listening to. Every outstanding person has been influenced in their career by a good, kind adult. Can you be a good, kind adult to at least one young person?

4. Give out your own golden lemons. If you come across a stupid act by an organization bestow on them your own 'Golden Lemon' award – an accolade celebrating their stupidity. Check out www.flexiblethinkingforum.org.uk to share your examples of stupidity.

5. Celebrate your stupidity. Every day you will add to your list of stupid things you have done. It is inevitable. Come to terms with it. Show humility. Have a hibris attitude state. It's fine being stupid so long as you learn from it and avoid 5 star stupidity.

Your dreams and DNA are unique - go out there and make a difference!

About the author

Apart from being stupid and responding to acts of stupidity in the world around him Andy Green spends his time sharing his skills. He unlocks creativity and unleashes communications for people and organizations he feels are important.

He is the author of 'Creativity in Public Relations', now in its third edition and translated into Chinese, Croatian, Indonesian, Korean, Latvian, Polish, and Russian. He is also the author of 'Effective Personal Communications Skills' on how each of us can transform our world through our communications, and 'A Minute with Tony Blair', inspired by a chance meeting with the former Prime Minister.

Andy has lectured and run training events around the world. He is the founder of creativity consultancy creativity@work and social enterprise the Flexible Thinking Forum. Andy is a partner with GREEN communications, and a director of the Wakefield Media and Creativity Centre.

Andy also promotes 'Blue Monday' to show how we can all overcome the most depressing day of the year (usually the third Monday in January.)

Andy Green is a Fellow of the Chartered Institute of Public Relations and recipient of the Institute's Sir Stephen Tallents medal for outstanding contribution to the public relations profession.

He lives on beautiful Barry Island, and works 240 miles away in Yorkshire. Which is stupid.

About the Information Commissioner's Office

From data protection and electronic communications to freedom of information and environmental regulations - the Information Commissioner's Office (ICO) is the UK's independent public body set up to protect personal information and promote public access to official information.

The ICO enforces and oversees the Data Protection Act, the Freedom of Information Act, the Environmental Information Regulations, and the Privacy and Electronic Communications Regulations.

Its main functions are educating and influencing (promoting good practice and giving information and advice), resolving problems (resolving eligible complaints from people who think their rights have been breached) and enforcing (using legal sanctions against those who ignore or refuse to accept their obligations).

Data protection law reinforces common sense rules of information handling and ensures organisations manage their personal information in a sensible way by keeping it up to date, only for as long as they need it for a specified purpose, and of course, must keep it secure.

Some organisations understandably err on the side of caution and do not release information when they could do so, using the Data Protection Act as an excuse not to do something, rather than seeing it as good business sense to treat their customers and their information with respect.

For more information about the ICO please visit their website www.ico.gov.uk

The website dispels many myths surrounding data protection including: *'Data Protection stops you from taking photos in schools', 'The Data Protection Act means a company is never allowed to give a customer's details to a third party", 'The Data Protection Act stops parents from finding out their children's exam results', 'The Data Protection Act prevents the releases of offender's details to victims', and even 'The Data Protection Act prevents priests from naming sick parishioners during church prayers'.*

The Flexible Thinking Forum is grateful for financial support provided by the ICO in its work.

Index

Thank you

No man is an island. No book or campaign is a singular effort.

Thanks go to:
Sue and Robert at the Information Commissioner's Office

Steve Davies – his good sense and invaluable knowledge of 'Stupid law'

Marcus Dyson of eleventeenth for ignoring the stupidity of giving my ideas on-line support

Richard Jones at Tangent Publishing for making the book happen

Steve McDermott – for his inspiration and celebration of 'failure'

Amanda Marsh – her torch continues to shine

David Rattray – for manning 'the Scottish office' and beyond

Barry Sheerman MP – a lifelong tutor

Douglas Smith – for helping me fight institutional stupidity

Everyone who helped make Stupid Aid 2007 possible – and for those who stood in the way, may they reflect on what they missed out on.

Charlotte for accompanying her dad on the Stupid Aid tour in 2007 (despite her describing her role as being the equivalent to the character of Lynne in 'Alan Partridge') and Lizzie – sorry I made you feel uncomfortable in the supermarket queue.

The team of beta readers including Anne Akers, Cliff Arnall, Jackie Le Fevre, Dave Marsh, Alan Preece, Geoff Roberts and Heather Yaxley.

The team at GREEN communications for putting up with a stupid colleague.

For all the clients who has shown faith in me

Anyone who has had to suffer stupidity from me.

And finally, the waitress who wouldn't slice me a lemon, and inspired me to take on the world.

The story behind Stupid Aid

I had a stupid idea. A singularly stupid idea. I was getting fed up with what I perceived to be a growth in stupidity in the world around me. I had coined the term 'compound stupidity' to describe this phenomenon.

In February 2007 I completed a speaking tour of Australia, often doing two or three events in one day. I had earlier literally created a vehicle for my creativity consultancy work, 'the world's smallest conference centre', a two-seater car to cater for 1:1 consultations at conferences and special events. (I once had four Australian girls in the car at one time at a conference in Belfast, a delegate lost their umbrella in it, as well as hosting luminaries such as the government minister Ed Balls and renowned architect Will Alsop.)

In my study and teaching of creativity I believe flexible thinking is at the heart of creative thinking. I was also developing my expertise in word of mouth communications and was sensitive to the need to brand and make any message sticky. I knew from experience that you may need a legitimizer to help sanction an idea which might be regarded as outrageous.

Earlier in 2007 I had delivered a well-received talk at a business network group raising funds for the children's charity Barnardo's.

I was also a Fellow of the Chartered Institute of Public Relations and had joined the Chartered Institute of Marketing.

Like any idea, it is an amalgam of many other ideas orbiting around you, coalescing into a coherent concept.

My idea was to do something about the increase in stupidity by doing a one week tour of the UK delivering 14 events over five days, with 2 or 3 lectures a day, travelling in my conference centre, working in partnership with the Institutes of Marketing and Public Relations, with profits from the events going to Barnardo's, and branding the initiative 'Stupid Aid – make stupidity history'*.

So, in September 2007 the first Stupid Aid week was launched – and the rest is history.

The idea spawned this book and also the creation of the Flexible Thinking Forum to provide a sustainable vehicle to promote creative thinking skills.

For details about the future of the Forum and its activities, and how you can become a Stupid Aid Ambassador, please visit: www.flexiblethinkingforum.org.uk

(*Actually, we will never make stupidity history as we believe in the prevalence of 1, 2 and 3 star stupidity. The word of mouth and publicity value of the phrase 'make stupidity history' and its resonance with other crusade campaigns was felt to outweigh its technical inaccuracy.)

Further reading/links

Stupidity
The following are recommended for their insight or approach to understanding stupidity.
'Why smart people can be so stupid' Robert J. Sternberg
'The Black Swan' Nassim Nicholas Taleb
'Dumbth' Steve Allen
'The Natural History of Stupidity' Paul Tabori
'The story of stupidity' James F. Welles

Creative/Flexible thinking
I have limited myself to a selection of favourite/useful texts:
'The Act of Creation' Arthur Koestler
'Handbook of Creativity' Robert J. Sternberg
'Weird ideas that work' Robert I. Sutton
'How to get ideas' Jack Foster
'Flow' Mihaly Csikszentmihalyi
'The Creative Habit' Twyla Tharp
Anything by Michael Michalko

Reciprocal altruism
'The Selfish Gene' Richard Dawkins

Viral/meme communications
'*Jump start your business brain*' Doug Hall
'*The Tipping Point*' Malcolm Gladwell
'*The book of Gossage*' Howard Gossage
Anything by Seth Godin

Also by the author
'*Creativity in Public Relations*' Kogan Page
'*Effective Personal Communications*' Kogan Page
'*A Minute with Tony Blair*' Pontefract Press

For more references visit
www.flexiblethinkingforum.org.uk